DONNA ABELA is an award-winning playwright. Her play *Jump For Jordan* won the 2013 Griffin Playwriting Award and the 2015 Australian Writers' Guild's AWGIE Award for Stage. It is on the HSC Drama Syllabus, was one of three Australian plays presented in Spanish at the 2018 Women Playwright's International Conference in Santiago de Chile, and was the creative component of her 2016 doctoral thesis entitled *Dialogic Interplay: a Strategy for Representing Difference and Cultural Diversity on Stage*. Other recent plays include *Monkey ... Journey to the West* (2014 Brisbane Festival, 2015 Melbourne Festival, 2015 Sydney Opera House programs), *Spirit* (2016 AWGIE Award for Radio), *Aurora's Lament* (2012 AWGIE Award for Radio), and *Mrs Macquarie's Cello* (2010 AWGIE Award for Radio). Donna supports the development of new performance works, and leads processes that leverage the creative proficiency and resilience of writers. In the past year, she has taught, mentored or provided dramaturgy to over a hundred students, emerging and professional writers for screen and stage. She is a founding member and board member of PYT | Fairfield. Along with Vanessa Bates, Hilary Bell, Noëlle Janaczeska, Verity Laughton, Ned Manning and Cath Zimdahl, she is also a founding member of 7-ON, a playwrights' alliance which advocates for playwrights and initiates production and publishing projects.

Acting students from the Charles Sturt University production of TALES FROM THE ARABIAN NIGHTS *in 2017. (Photo: Haley Kotzur)*

TALES

from the

ARABIAN NIGHTS

adapted from the classic tales by

DONNA ABELA

CURRENCY PRESS
The performing arts publisher

CURRENCY PLAYS

First published in 2019
by Currency Press Pty Ltd,
PO Box 2287, Strawberry Hills, NSW, 2012, Australia
enquiries@currency.com.au
www.currency.com.au

Typeset by Dean Nottle for Currency Press.
Cover image shows The Rhode Island Panel. Photograph by Timothy Crutchett, courtesy Sam Bowker, Charles Sturt University.
Cover design by Alissa Dinallo for Currency Press.

A catalogue record for this book is available from the National Library of Australia

Contents

Currency Press acknowledges the Traditional Owners of the Country on which we live and work. We pay our respects to all Aboriginal and Torres Strait Islander Elders, past and present.

Acting students from the Charles Sturt University production of TALES FROM THE ARABIAN NIGHTS *in 2017. (Photo: Haley Kotzur)*

INTRODUCTION

Donna Abela's *Tales from the Arabian Nights* is an adaptation of a recent translation into English by Husain Haddawy of *The Arabian Nights*. The original work is a collection of tales full of mystery, wonder and adventure from across Arabia, Persia, India and Greece. While there is no attributed source, the originating fourteenth-century manuscript of stories for this play was edited by the Iraqi-American scholar Muhsin Mahdi. By the eighteenth century, *The Arabian Nights* had been popularised in Europe through Antoine Galland's French version.

The original collection depicts a king who decides the only way to be sure of a wife's fidelity is to spend one night only with her and the next day to decapitate her and marry a new wife. The latest wife in a long line decides to tell the king stories in an attempt to delay her execution for as long as possible—a thousand and one nights.

Abela overlays this central plot with the current political situation of our treatment of refugees. In Abela's play, the paranoid King Shahrayar has built a wall that keeps both refugees and terrorists out. For safety, he kills everyone and everything that is a potential threat. At the opening of the play, the king has beheaded his queen. She had hidden refugees, known as the Smuggles, in the kingdom, but the king has locked them up and vowed to execute one each day at dawn.

Disguised as the next refugee due for execution, the daughter of a courtier, Shahrazad, bravely steps in and begins a tale that continues into another and another in a bid to save the Smuggles' lives. Shahrazad tells these tales with what Abela describes as 'the insistence of the bazaar and the ingenuity of the nomad' to weave compassion into the heart of the king, intriguing him until he is utterly transformed. The storyteller changes the king and in so doing, the world.

The target audience is young but Abela deftly avoids a juvenile or Disney approach in this play. The directness of the language helps get under the political subterfuge and fear mongering perpetrated by the despotic king, revealing the essential questions of compassion and empathy posed by these stories.

Abela's ability to make something appear simple yet reverberate with multiple layers of meaning is shown firstly through her selection of tales for this play. Marvel and horror run side by side in a conspicuous metaphor for the current plight of refugees and the fear that 'terrorists' might overtake the country at any moment. The parallel with current Australian and world politics is evident—King Shahrayar's paranoid worldview is akin to something we might see on the nightly news.

The Smuggles—who also act as the chorus from which all the other stories emerge—try to break through the king's wall but are constantly pushed back. We are left asking, how can we allow this?

The story-filled nights start with the queen's beheading—and the severed head continuing to talk—and continue with a flying monster, an ape stranded at sea, humans who turn into dogs, and one who turns into a deer. Fish sing and dance as they transform back into the people they once were. The rhythm of the incredible stories is measured by the repetition of dawn and dusk in a street scene outside the palace, and the call to prayer. Power is subverted for a moment when the fisherman sits on the king's throne. For that brief moment, like All Fools' Day in medieval Europe when the fool becomes king for a day, the lowest is seen as the highest and the king becomes disoriented. He begins to crack.

The gruesome story of Qasim, who is quartered by the bandits, followed by the story of the torching of forty thieves in oil jars by Ali Baba's daughter, shock the king. The stories have a cumulative effect until the king's heart is penetrated, he cracks wide open, falls in love with Shahrazad and finally brings down the wall of fear—literally and metaphorically.

The play is a dream for designers and actors. It requires everyone to work together imaginatively to bring forth the images of demons, transformations, slayings, oceans and deserts into the theatrical space. A great deal of the conjuring is done through Abela's language and the way it contrasts with the surrounding mayhem. Abela's ability to find still points in this turning world, such as the repetition of dawn and dusk and the graveyard scenes, offer us much-needed moments of reflection. The soundscape of the play is critical.

The way the actors change quickly from role to role telling stories within stories is what makes this play challenging and fun. Originally written for six actors playing many roles, more recently *Tales from the*

Arabian Nights has had productions with larger casts. The chorus of Smuggles is a powerful element that adds light and shade to the entire play and is a key element in the design. What is so inspiring in this play is the way the stories resound with and within each other. As you come to understand one story it helps you understand something more about another, and so the process gets richer and deeper.

In the Charles Sturt University production of the play, it was an actor playing the sea captain who brought home the crux of the play. In rehearsal I had skipped over the importance of a line offering assistance to those in distress and the actor brought it to light through the directness and seriousness of his delivery. The sea captain reaches out of his boat to save the ape stranded at sea, telling his crew and the world, 'Ah! God's creatures is all the same to me. Particularly one in distress. Welcome aboard, matey!'

Written in the aftermath of the Tampa affair, when the *MV Tampa* was refused entry into Australian waters after the ship's Norwegian captain rescued hundreds of asylum seekers from drowning at sea, *Tales from The Arabian Nights* reminds us that ape or human, resident or refugee, we are all the same in times of great need.

Dominique Sweeney
February 2019

Dominique Sweeney lectures in Stage and Screen Acting at Charles Sturt University. He is a performer, creator and film-maker specialising in documenting performance practice. In particular he researches and documents traditional Aboriginal public performances and works with Traditional Owners on how best to manage digital archives.

Acting students from the Charles Sturt University production of TALES FROM THE ARABIAN NIGHTS *in 2017. (Photo: Haley Kotzur)*

Tales from the Arabian Nights was commissioned and first produced by Kim Carpenter's Theatre of Image at the Laycock Street Theatre, Gosford, on 20 May 2004, with the following cast:

KING SHAHRAYAR, KING YUNAN, KING OF BAGHDAD	Nicholas Papademetriou
SMUGGLE, SHAHRAZAD, FIRST DEMON, PEASANT, COLOURED FISH, MAJANA, KING OF BAGHDAD'S DAUGHTER	Felicity Price
SMUGGLE, MOB, DINARZAD, MAN WITH TWO DOGS, YOUNG BULL, YOUNG MAN, PEASANT, ADVISER TO KING YUNAN, CALLIGRAPHER, APE	Lenka Kripic
SMUGGLE, QUEEN SAHAR, SHEPHERDESS, BEGGAR GIRL, SHE-DEMON, PROFESSOR DUBAN, COLOURED FISH, ALI BABA, TAILOR, MESSENGER, THIRD DEMON, FINAL DEMON	Amie McKenna
SMUGGLE, FIRST EXECUTIONER, SHOPKEEPER, DOGBROTHER, FISHERMAN, PEASANT, SECOND EXECUTIONER, BANDIT CAPTAIN, HIGHWAY ROBBER, MERCHANT, FINAL DEMON	Matt Edgerton
SMUGGLE, ADVISER, MAN WITH A DEER, DOGBROTHER, SECOND DEMON, PEASANT, QASIM, BANDIT, SEA CAPTAIN, HIGHWAY ROBBER, FINAL DEMON	Steve Vella

Director, Patrick Nolan
Composer, Oonagh Sherrard
Designer, Kim Carpenter
Choreographer, Pamela French
Stage Manager, Roger Press
ASM / Puppeteer, Gavin Pawsey
Lighting Designer, Jo Elliott
Cultural Consultant, Maha Ismail

CHARACTERS

KING SHAHRAYAR (pronounced: Shahrayaar)
QUEEN SAHAR (pronounced: Sahhar)
ADVISER
FIRST EXECUTIONER
MOB AT COURT
SHAHRAZAD (pronounced: Shahrazaad)
DINARZAD (pronounced: Deenarzaad)
SMUGGLES LOCKED IN SEWER
SHOPKEEPER
A MAN WITH A DEER
A MAN WITH TWO BLACK DOGS
FIRST DEMON
DEER
SHEPHERDESS
YOUNG BULL / YOUNG MAN
FIRST DOGBROTHER
SECOND DOGBROTHER
PEOPLE OF THE HARBOUR
BEGGAR GIRL / SHE-DEMON
FISHERMAN
SECOND DEMON
KING YUNAN (pronounced: Yunaan)
PROFESSOR DUBAN (pronounced: Dubaan)
PEASANTS
ADVISER TO KING YUNAN
SECOND EXECUTIONER
FOUR COLOURED FISH
ALI BABA
QASIM (pronounced: Qaasim or Carsim)
BANDIT CAPTAIN
40 BANDITS

MAJANA (pronounced: Majaana)
KING OF BAGHDAD
CALLIGRAPHER / APE
KING OF BAGHDAD'S DAUGHTER
HIGHWAY ROBBERS
TAILOR / THIRD DEMON
SEA CAPTAIN
MERCHANT
MESSENGER
FINAL DEMON

The play was originally performed by six actors. However, it can be performed by a larger cast.

NOTES FOR PRODUCTION

This stage adaptation attempts to capture the spirit of its source document: *The Arabian Nights* translated by Husain Haddawy (1990), and based on the text of the fourteenth-century Syrian manuscript edited by Muhsin Mahdi (1984). In this translation, every storyteller is a merchant who trades stories for a favour, a delay, or to save a life. Every story has currency, is taken seriously, and never fails to amaze. Importantly, storytellers respect the intelligence of their listener, satisfying and humanising them with their dignity intact. We are in the robust world of the bazaar, not literally, but dynamically. This dynamic is the attitude of this script's aesthetic: interactive, negotiable, transformative, and polyphonous.

Using only their bodies and clothing, or what they can grab from the king's chamber, the Smuggles create the landscape for each tale. They become characters, create puppets and props, and make sounds and music. They are never idle, always engrossed in performing, accompanying, or listening. They are the means by which Shahrazad insinuates her stories into the king's mind and heart. They are the insistence of the bazaar, and the ingenuity of the nomad, thwarting the king's mood for incarceration and division.

NOTE ON PRONUNCIATION

In Arabic words all R's are rolled, as in the Spanish language (not French), only slightly shorter. Every letter is pronounced; there are no silent letters.

This script was developed with the support of Playworks Women Performance Writers Network and the Australian National Playwrights' Centre.

King Shahrayar's court.

Through cracks in the wall, the faces of SMUGGLES *appear one by one. The* SMUGGLES *bang on the wall, more and more insistently until, like their hope, their protest fades to nothing, and they disappear back into the shadows.*

QUEEN SAHAR *stands trial. The* ADVISER *reads the charges to* KING SHAHRAYAR *and the* MOB. *An* EXECUTIONER *is at the ready.*

ADVISER: Queen Sahar. You were caught under the palace smuggling outsiders into the kingdom.

MOB: Foreign riffraff!

KING SHAHRAYAR: You are the ringleader of a smuggling ring! Our nosing around has proved it.

ADVISER: Yes. Therefore, by the law of King Shahrayar, you are charged with being an Official Troublemaker …

MOB: A smuggler of Smuggles!

KING SHAHRAYAR: … and sentenced to death.

ADVISER: My Queen. You may say one thing in your defence.

KING SHAHRAYAR: Why did you help the Smuggles?!

QUEEN SAHAR: I found them eating grass…

MOB: Strangers are strange!

QUEEN SAHAR: … saw them at our border, looking back at their burning churches and mosques …

MOB: Strangers are dangerous!

QUEEN SAHAR: … robbed by bandits, with nothing left except the clothes on their backs. It cost nothing to open the gate and let them soak up the sun.

MOB: But they've got nits and lice and pimples and germs!

KING SHAHRAYAR: And they're here, in my kingdom, uninvited!

QUEEN SAHAR: In need of help.

MOB: The queen helped the Smuggles! Down with the Smuggles!

KING SHAHRAYAR: Yes. Down with the Smuggles. Each night, one Smuggle must be brought to my chamber. I will torment them, make them obey, but when the call of dawn is heard, I will have their head chopped off. I, King Shahrayar, vow to do this until every last Smuggle is dead.

ADVISER: But My Lord, O King.

KING SHAHRAYAR: What?!

ADVISER: The dungeon is full to the brim. To kill the Smuggles one by one will take years.

KING SHAHRAYAR: My fury will outlive the lot of them! I've tried everything, but they keep coming, a tsunami of Smuggles flooding into my kingdom!

MOB: With nits and lice and pimples and germs! And big noses! And pongy breath! And odd names! And rotten luck!

KING SHAHRAYAR: Let them rot in the dungeon until their number is up.

MOB: They'll breed like rabbits!

QUEEN SAHAR: O unhappy King. The spell of the wrong story has turned you into a beast.

KING SHAHRAYAR: And you have betrayed me! Your king and husband! Prepare for your death!

QUEEN SAHAR: Spare me and God will spare you.

KING SHAHRAYAR: Executioner!

QUEEN SAHAR: Destroy me and God will destroy you.

KING SHAHRAYAR: Proceed.

The EXECUTIONER *takes the* QUEEN *to the chopping block.*

QUEEN SAHAR: You are warned.

KING SHAHRAYAR: Off with her head!

The EXECUTIONER *beheads the* QUEEN. *Her head floats into the air and sings.*

QUEEN SAHAR: [*singing*] I don't trust the days
    I hope things will change
    But I can't see the time
    When clouds of doubt will go
    We are now
    Left hanging
    Like our future.

The QUEEN*'s head disappears into a crack in the wall.*

Transition into ...

A cemetery containing hundreds of headstones.

The ADVISER *holds a bundle of clothes and pats the dirt on a freshly dug grave. His daughters,* SHAHRAZAD *and* DINARZAD, *are with him.*

ADVISER: Another beheading of someone who needed help… another day of Smuggles locked up in the dungeon… another year of the king's terrible revenge. It's got to stop.

SHAHRAZAD: Father?

ADVISER: Yes, Shahrazad?

SHAHRAZAD: I can stop the king.

ADVISER: How?

SHAHRAZAD: Give me those clothes.

ADVISER: These? These belonged to the Smuggle. The one we just buried.

SHAHRAZAD: Let me put them on. Then take me to the king and present me as the next Smuggle due to die.

ADVISER: No. He'll torment you all night, make you obey him, and when the call of dawn is heard, he'll have your head chopped off.

SHAHRAZAD: Only if I don't succeed.

ADVISER: Shahrazad. Count the tombstones. Hundreds of Smuggles have been killed already. What can you do that's different?

SHAHRAZAD: With my sister's help, I will tell stories, strange and amazing stories, that will make the king open his heart and offer the Smuggles his protection.

ADVISER: This is quite a boast.

DINARZAD: But father, Shahrazad reads Greek, Persian, Turkish, Arabic and Hebrew. She's studied science, philosophy and history. She knows poetry and the healing lore of plants. She's full of stories! Her plan might work.

SHAHRAZAD: Dinarzad? Will you come with me?

DINARZAD: Yes.

ADVISER: Shahrazad. If you go to the king disguised as a Smuggle, and if you fail to amaze him with your stories and open his heart, since I cannot disobey him, I will have no choice but to put you to death.

SHAHRAZAD: I know.

> The ADVISER *hands* SHAHRAZAD *the clothes, and embraces his daughters.*

ADVISER: My sweet, wise, wonderful daughters. May God not take you from me.

SHAHRAZAD: Let's go.

Transition into ...

King Shahrayar's opulent chamber:

KING SHAHRAYAR *sits on his throne surrounded by food, wine, riches and splendour.* SHAHRAZAD *and* DINARZAD *wear Smuggle clothes.* SHAHRAZAD *stands before* KING SHAHRAYAR. DINARZAD *waits.*

KING SHAHRAYAR: So, Smuggle! Have you finished digging your own grave?

SHAHRAZAD: Yes, My King.

KING SHAHRAYAR: Have you carved your name onto your tombstone?

SHAHRAZAD: Yes, My King.

KING SHAHRAYAR: Have you sharpened the executioner's axe?

SHAHRAZAD: Yes, My King.

KING SHAHRAYAR: Good. All this tormenting wears me out. You may rest. Do as you please until daybreak announces your death.

SHAHRAZAD: Thank you, My King.

DINARZAD: Shahrazad, if you're not sleepy, tell us one of your lovely tales to while away the night.

KING SHAHRAYAR: What?

SHAHRAZAD: Good King Shahrayar. With your permission, may I tell a story?

KING SHAHRAYAR: A story? A story. Yes, alright. But no funny business. You'll still die at dawn, as I have vowed.

Sitting on his throne, KING SHAHRAYAR *eats and drinks.*

SHAHRAZAD: Thank you, my King ... *Listen!*

At this word, the SMUGGLES *timidly sneak out of the cracks in the walls, and insinuate their way into 'The Tale of The Merchant and the Demon'.*

I heard, O happy King, that once, a shopkeeper ...

SHAHRAZAD *invites a* SMUGGLE *to become a* SHOPKEEPER.

... was sitting in an orchard. He had a heavy heart, tears in his eyes, and his burial clothes in his lap. Soon, a man with a deer ...

She invites another SMUGGLE *to become a* MAN WITH A DEER.

... and a man with two black dogs ...

DINARZAD *becomes a* MAN WITH TWO BLACK DOGS.

… walked by the orchard. They waved at the shopkeeper, in case he needed help. But just then, a whirlwind rose out of the dust. And out of the dust came a thunderous voice…

SHAHRAZAD *becomes the* FIRST DEMON.

FIRST DEMON: Prepare for your death!

The MAN WITH A DEER *and the* MAN WITH TWO DOGS *grab their animals and dive under the* SHOPKEEPER'*s shroud. They quake and cling to each other.*

MAN WITH TWO DOGS: What was that?

MAN WITH A DEER: Is it human?

MAN WITH TWO DOGS: Will it eat me?

MAN WITH A DEER: Who are you? Are you mad?

SHOPKEEPER: I'm a shopkeeper.

MAN WITH A DEER: This orchard is haunted!

SHOPKEEPER: I know.

MAN WITH A DEER: By demons!

SHOPKEEPER: Big demons, huge, so enormous that when they walk, their heads make the clouds swish. I know. I've got an appointment with one.

MAN WITH TWO DOGS: What?

MAN WITH A DEER: When?

SHOPKEEPER: Now!

The FIRST DEMON *seizes the* SHOPKEEPER, *shakes him, and throws him to the ground.*

FIRST DEMON: Shopkeeper! This time last year, in this orchard, you killed my little son!

SHOPKEEPER: Accidentally.

FIRST DEMON: Walloped him.

SHOPKEEPER: With a tiny, weeny pip.

FIRST DEMON: You were spitting pips left, right and everywhere.

SHOPKEEPER: Because, demon, there's no sign up. There shoulda been signs. 'Haunted Orchard. Demons Cross Here'. Then I woulda been careful, and not spat a seed at your son's noggin and killed him.

FIRST DEMON: Have you settled your affairs?

SHOPKEEPER: Yes.

FIRST DEMON: Have you kissed your wife and kids goodbye?
SHOPKEEPER: Yes.
FIRST DEMON: Have you brought your burial clothes with you?
SHOPKEEPER: Yes.
FIRST DEMON: Then prepare for your death!

The FIRST DEMON *lifts the* SHOPKEEPER *into the air.* KING SHAHRAYAR *enjoys this.*

MAN WITH A DEER: Wait! Mr Demon, king of the demons, scariest of the scariest demons! How you doing? Allow me to introduce my wife.

He gestures towards the DEER.

FIRST DEMON: Wife?
MAN WITH A DEER: Yes.
FIRST DEMON: That's a deer.
MAN WITH A DEER: Yes. It's our wedding anniversary soon. Fifty years together.
FIRST DEMON: Has your wife always been a deer?
MAN WITH A DEER: Well … Demon. If I tell you my story, and if you find it strange and amazing, more strange and amazing than what's happened to you and this shopkeeper, will you grant me half of this shopkeeper's life?
FIRST DEMON: Very well…

The DEMON *lowers the* SHOPKEEPER.

… but this better be good.
MAN WITH A DEER: *Listen!*

At this word, the SMUGGLES *and* DINARZAD *prepare to insinuate themselves into 'The Tale of the Man with a Deer'.*

My wife, this deer, couldn't have any kids. We tried and tried, but we just weren't blessed with any. So, on my wife's say-so, I took a second wife, and with her, I finally had a baby, a boy, with eyes as bright as the moon. But when my baby boy became a handsome young man, all of a sudden, he went missing. Demon, the heartache. I looked everywhere for my son, and blubbered and bawled for months, until the Great Feast Day was coming and I had to stop and get everything ready. Shepherdess!

A SMUGGLE *becomes the* SHEPHERDESS.

SHEPHERDESS: Yes, boss?

MAN WITH A DEER: Bring me a nice young bull to slaughter for the feast.

SHEPHERDESS: Yes, boss.

> DINARZAD *becomes the* YOUNG BULL.

How 'bout this one?

MAN WITH A DEER: His eyes are as bright as the moon. But he's plump enough. Hold him still.

> *The* MAN WITH A DEER *raises his knife. The* YOUNG BULL *bucks and bellows.*

YOUNG BULL: Dad, Dad, don't do it!

MAN WITH A DEER: Shepherdess?

SHEPHERDESS: Yes, boss?

MAN WITH A DEER: I suspect something.

SHEPHERDESS: That's because this bull's not a real bull. It looks like a bull. But it's not, it's your son.

MAN WITH A DEER: My son?

SHEPHERDESS: Your wife got real jealous. Put a spell on him and turned him into a bull. I'm good at magic and stuff, so I can detect these things.

MAN WITH A DEER: My boy … is a bull?

> *The* MAN WITH A DEER *weeps and hugs the* YOUNG BULL. *The* YOUNG BULL *bellows.*

SHEPHERDESS: I can change him back, if you want, into a man.

MAN WITH A DEER: Yes, please! Do it!

SHEPHERDESS: On two conditions.

MAN WITH A DEER: Anything.

SHEPHERDESS: I want to marry him, your son. He's cute. Nice eyes. Not now, but. After, when he's not a bull. I don't wanna marry a bull.

MAN WITH A DEER: Okay. But what's the second condition?

SHEPHERDESS: I want to give your wife a taste her own medicine. Turn her into a deer. A deer's pretty, not ugly and angry, which is what she's gonna be, when this bull's your son again. She's gonna freak.

MAN WITH A DEER: Okay. I agree. Now please, change him back.

> *The* SHEPHERDESS *utters an incantation.*

SHEPHERDESS: If this bull is a real bull
Let him stay a bull
But if this bull is under a spell
Let him change back
By the will of the Creator of Everything.

The YOUNG BULL *shakes and changes back into a* YOUNG MAN.

YOUNG MAN: Dad!
MAN WITH A DEER: My son!

The MAN WITH A DEER *and the* YOUNG MAN *embrace.*

The SMUGGLES *and* DINARZAD *resume their characters in 'The Tale of the Merchant and the Demon'.*

So, demon, my son who was a bull, married the shepherdess who did magic and turned my wife into this deer. Is my story stranger and more amazing than what happened to you and the shopkeeper?
FIRST DEMON: Yes.
MAN WITH A DEER: Will you grant me half of the shopkeeper's life?
FIRST DEMON: I will. But I still have to kill the other half.

The FIRST DEMON *grabs the* SHOPKEEPER *and raises him into the air.*

Get ready to die!
MAN WITH TWO DOGS: Mr Demon, king of the demons, scariest of the scariest demons! Allow me to introduce my two brothers.

He gestures towards the two DOGS.

FIRST DEMON: Your brothers are dogs?
MAN WITH TWO DOGS: At the moment, yes.
FIRST DEMON: What happened?
MAN WITH TWO DOGS: Demon. If I tell you my story, and if you find it strange and amazing, more strange and amazing than what happened to you and this shopkeeper, will you grant me the other half of the shopkeeper's life?
FIRST DEMON: Very well…

The DEMON *releases the* SHOPKEEPER.

… but this also better be good.
MAN WITH TWO DOGS: For six years, me and my two brothers, we worked in the Grand Bazaar…

A rooster crows. Dawn breaks.

The city outside bustles into action: traffic rumbles, vendors spruik, radios blare, and children play.

The SMUGGLES *freeze, drop their characters, and scurry back through the cracks in the wall.*

KING SHAHRAYAR: Then what happened?

DINARZAD: Shahrazad! What a strange and lovely story!

SHAHRAZAD: Yes. But it's nothing compared to what I will tell you tonight… if the king spares me and lets me live.

KING SHAHRAYAR: What?

SHAHRAZAD: It will be even more amazing!

KING SHAHRAYAR: [*aside*] By God, if I kill this Smuggle, I won't know what happened to the shopkeeper and the demon and the man with two dogs. What will I do?

The EXECUTIONER *enters, with his axe, to kill* SHAHRAZAD. *The* ADVISER *enters, with a burial shroud, to collect* SHAHRAZAD's *body.* SHAHRAZAD *and* DINARZAD *tremble in a corner.*

Transition into …

The first daytime interlude:

We are inside the nightmarish recesses of KING SHAHRAYAR's *mind as he is haunted by elements of the stories he has just heard. He imagines a bull snorting and preparing to charge at him. He imagines fighting the bull with the shroud. He hears the distorted sounds of a bull bellowing, the shopkeeper weeping, and the words: 'Is it human? I still have to kill. Dad, Dad, don't do it!'*

Transition into …

The next night.

KING SHAHRAYAR: Smuggle. You may live for one more night.

The EXECUTIONER *and the* ADVISER *exit.*

But in the morning, God Almighty willing, I will put you to death.

SHAHRAZAD: Thank you, My King.

DINARZAD: Shahrazad. If you're not too sleepy, finish the story of the shopkeeper and the demon and the man with two dogs.

SHAHRAZAD: With the greatest pleasure… *Listen!*

At this word, the SMUGGLES *sneak out of the cracks in the walls, and insinuate their way into 'The Tale of The Man with Two Dogs'.* DINARZAD *becomes the* MAN WITH TWO DOGS.

MAN WITH TWO DOGS: For six years, me and my two brothers, we worked in the Grand Bazaar. We had shops side by side each other. I liked my shop, selling figs and oranges, keeping count of things. But my brothers were restless gambling pisspots. Every spring, they took me aside and said …

Two SMUGGLES *become the* DOGBROTHERS.

FIRST DOGBROTHER: Come on!

SECOND DOGBROTHER: Scaredy bum.

FIRST DOGBROTHER: A whole year off. What's wrong with ya?

SECOND DOGBROTHER: Travelling the world, selling stuff.

FIRST DOGBROTHER: Making money.

SECOND DOGBROTHER: Meeting girlies.

FIRST DOGBROTHER: Lock your shop up, come on. Let's embark on a big brotherly adventure!

MAN WITH TWO DOGS: For six years they begged me, and for six years I said no. But then I finally gave in and said yes. Brothers! I'm ready! How much money have you saved up for the trip?

SECOND DOGBROTHER: Heaps.

FIRST DOGBROTHER: Not much.

SECOND DOGBROTHER: Nothing.

FIRST DOGBROTHER: But if you sold all the figs and oranges in your shop …

SECOND DOGBROTHER: And all the pots and plates and furniture in your house …

FIRST DOGBROTHER: You won't need them.

SECOND DOGBROTHER: Not on a trip.

FIRST DOGBROTHER: Then we could all afford to go away …

SECOND DOGBROTHER: For a whole year.

FIRST DOGBROTHER: Excellent.

SECOND DOGBROTHER: Go on.

FIRST DOGBROTHER: Sell everything you own.

MAN WITH TWO DOGS: So I did. I buried half the money, in case we came back poor and penniless, and with the other half, I hired a ship, and loaded it up with merchandise.

They load the ship and sing.

DOGBROTHERS: [*singing*] Smelly spices
           Silky tassels
           Fancy fabric
           Comfy carpets.
  All aboard who are going aboard!

They sail the choppy sea. The DOGBROTHERS *are seasick.*

MAN WITH TWO DOGS: Look! The harbour of a foreign city! Let's drop anchor, and sell some of our merchandise.
FIRST DOGBROTHER: Yeah.
SECOND DOGBROTHER: Before I puke.

They drop anchor, grab merchandise, and disembark. Instantly, they are mobbed by PEOPLE OF THE HARBOUR *who buy everything and carry it off.*

FIRST DOGBROTHER: They cleaned us out!
SECOND DOGBROTHER: Bought the lot!
FIRST DOGBROTHER: Paid money.
SECOND DOGBROTHER: Lots of money.
MAN WITH TWO DOGS: Let's see. We made … a thousand per cent profit. Let's go and buy more goods to sell in another city.

A SMUGGLE *becomes a* BEGGAR GIRL.

BEGGAR GIRL: Sir? Look at me. I've got nothing. No food, no house. Just hope that you might help me.
MAN WITH TWO DOGS: Of course I'll help you. What can I do?
BEGGAR GIRL: Marry me. Take me home on this boat, and protect me from the storms of life. If you judge my words, not what I look like, I promise you, I will reward your kindness.
MAN WITH TWO DOGS: Marry you?

The MAN WITH TWO DOGS *looks at her. His heart flutters and he goes all gooey.*

Yes!

The DOGBROTHERS *cheer and sing half-heartedly as they load the boat with merchandise.*

DOGBROTHERS: [*singing*] Smelly spices
           Silky tassels

Fancy fabric
Comfy carpets.
All aboard who are going aboard!

The MAN WITH TWO DOGS *and the* BEGGAR GIRL *board the ship. They dance and twirl and fall asleep in each other's arms. The* DOGBROTHERS *raise the anchor, sail the choppy sea, and are seasick again.*

FIRST DOGBROTHER: I hate them.
SECOND DOGBROTHER: Freeloading on us.
FIRST DOGBROTHER: It stinks.
SECOND DOGBROTHER: It's not right.
FIRST DOGBROTHER: We should complain.
SECOND DOGBROTHER: We could mutiny!
FIRST DOGBROTHER: Turn into pirates.
SECOND DOGBROTHER: And get famous and put in books!
FIRST DOGBROTHER: And achieve our criminal potential.
SECOND DOGBROTHER: And get girlfriends.
FIRST DOGBROTHER: Yeah, girlfriends.
SECOND DOGBROTHER: Let's chuck 'em overboard.
FIRST DOGBROTHER: Yeah. Come on!

The DOGBROTHERS *throw the* MAN WITH TWO DOGS *and the* BEGGAR GIRL *overboard and sail away.* KING SHAHRAYAR *enjoys this.*

MAN WITH TWO DOGS: Help! My wife! Save her! Where is she?

The BEGGAR GIRL *transforms into a* SHE-DEMON.

BEGGAR GIRL: I'm here, hubby, saving you.
MAN WITH TWO DOGS: But, you're a…
BEGGAR GIRL: She-demon. And your loser brothers tried to drown us. Hold on, babe. Nice and tight.

The SHE-DEMON *grabs him and flies across the sea.*

MAN WITH TWO DOGS: Next thing, I'm in the air, with my wife who was a beggar who is now a she-demon flying me over the choppy sea and back to the roof of my house!

They land.

I didn't know I married a she-demon!

BEGGAR GIRL: I'm one of the good ones. When I saw you, I was lovestruck, baby. Totally gaga. I wanted your heart to throb and your head to spin, so I changed shape. When you didn't shun me in that beggar girl get-up, I knew you were a kind soul. I've rewarded your kindness by saving your life. But now, babe, I'm off to obliterate your brothers.

MAN WITH TWO DOGS: What?

BEGGAR GIRL: Sink their ship, let them gurgle and perish.

MAN WITH TWO DOGS: No! Please don't kill them.

BEGGAR GIRL: You were nearly shark lunch because of them.

MAN WITH TWO DOGS: They're still my brothers. And if I let you kill them, I'll be as bad as they are, won't I?

BEGGAR GIRL: Okay, pumpkin. I won't kill them.

KING SHAHRAYAR: But what *are* you going to do to them?

> The BEGGAR GIRL *utters an incantation.*

BEGGAR GIRL: If his brothers are good men
Let them stay men
But if his brothers are vicious and nasty
Let them change into dogs
By the will of the Creator of Everything.

> The DOGBROTHERS *run in on all fours as dogs. They weep and lick his feet.*

I will change them back. Meet me at the seashore, in ten years time. See ya then, dreamboat.

> The BEGGAR GIRL *flies away.*

MAN WITH TWO DOGS: Demon. I was on my way to the seashore to meet my wife who's a she-demon who'll turn these dogs back into men, when I met this shopkeeper, and this man with a deer. This is my story. Isn't it amazing? More strange and amazing than what happened to you and the shopkeeper?

> The FIRST DEMON *thinks about it.* KING SHAHRAYAR *shakes his head, but the* FIRST DEMON *is delighted.*

FIRST DEMON: By God, it is!

> KING SHAHRAYAR *is surprised.*

MAN WITH TWO DOGS: Will you grant me the other half of the shopkeeper's life?

FIRST DEMON: Yes. shopkeeper, your life has been bought with these amazing stories. I'm happy with this bargain… and you are free!

The SHOPKEEPER, *the* MAN WITH A DEER *and the* MAN WITH TWO DOGS *rejoice.* KING SHAHRAYAR *is perplexed.*

KING SHAHRAYAR: What?

The SMUGGLES *drop their characters and sneak back into the cracks in the wall.*

DINARZAD: Sister! What a lovely story!

SHAHRAZAD: Yes. But it's nothing compared to the story of the fisherman and the demon.

KING SHAHRAYAR: What was that?

DINARZAD: Shahrazad. If you're not sleepy, will you tell us the story of the fisherman and the demon?

SHAHRAZAD: With pleasure. I heard, O happy King, that once, a poor fisherman cast his net into the sea three times a day. One day, when he had cast his net, it suddenly became unusually heavy…

A rooster crows. Dawn breaks. The city outside bustles into action: traffic rumbles, vendors spruik, radios blare, children play.

KING SHAHRAYAR: Then what happened?

DINARZAD: Shahrazad! This sounds like an amazing story!

SHAHRAZAD: It is. I'll finish it tonight … if the king spares me and lets me live.

KING SHAHRAYAR: [*aside*] By God, if I kill her, I won't find out what the fisherman caught in his net. What will I do?

The EXECUTIONER *enters with his axe. The* ADVISER *enters with a burial shroud.* SHAHRAZAD *and* DINARZAD *cower in a corner.*

Transition into …

The second daytime interlude:

We are inside the nightmarish recesses of KING SHAHRAYAR*'s mind, as he is haunted by elements of the stories he has just heard. He imagines a vicious dog attacking him, seizing his goblet and running away with it. He hears the distorted sounds of dogs barking, and the words: '… hate … obliterate … I'm happy with this …'*

Transition into …

The next night.

KING SHAHRAYAR: Smuggle. You are free to live one more night. One.

    The EXECUTIONER *and the* ADVISER *exit.*

But in the morning, God Almighty willing, I will put you to death. I will.

SHAHRAZAD: Thank you, My King.

DINARZAD: Shahrazad. If you're not too sleepy, tell us one of your lovely tales to while away the night.

KING SHAHRAYAR: Yes. The one about the fisherman and the demon.

SHAHRAZAD: With the greatest pleasure… *Listen!*

    At this word, the SMUGGLES *sneak out of the cracks in the walls, and insinuate their way into 'The Tale of The Fisherman and the Demon'.*

    A SMUGGLE *becomes a* FISHERMAN*, singing as he casts his net.*

FISHERMAN: [*singing*] I cast my net
        Into the sea
        For the first time
        What will I find?

    Another SMUGGLE *puts something under the net. The* FISHERMAN *tugs on it.*

What's this? Trouble, knowing my luck. Be nice if it was fulla fish. Might be fish. Might be a jackpot!

    The FISHERMAN *opens the net and finds a dead donkey.*

A donkey! Dead and smelly! Blast!

    The FISHERMAN *pushes the dead donkey out, and casts his net again.*

    [*Singing*] I cast my net
        Into the sea
        For the second time
        What will I find?

    The SMUGGLE *places something else under the net. The* FISHERMAN *tugs on it.*

More trouble. Probably caught a cold. Or a wave, maybe I caught a wave. Step back. Maybe I caught fire!

The FISHERMAN *opens the net to find rusty pots and pans.*

Bugger. I coulda sold these, if they weren't rusty. There's gotta be a silver lining but, somewhere in that sea…

The FISHERMAN *prays.*

O, God. I'm having a pretty bad trot. If you could let the sea swoosh something good into my net, something to eat, or something to sell, then I'd really be very grateful.

The FISHERMAN *casts his net. The* SMUGGLE *cautiously gestures to a wine bottle and looks imploringly at* KING SHAHRAYAR. *The* KING *hesitates at first, then allows the* SMUGGLE *to take it and place it under the net.*

> [*Singing*] I cast my net
> Into the sea
> For the third time
> What will I find?

The FISHERMAN *opens the net and finds a shiny bottle.*

Yes! This is more like it! This'll fetch a pretty price at the market. Once I make it shiny, tip the gunk out …

The FISHERMAN *tries to pull out the stopper. He pulls harder, eventually prising it out. The bottle shakes. A column of smoke rises from it, becoming the* SECOND DEMON, *played by another* SMUGGLE.

SECOND DEMON: Rejoice and be glad! For soon, you will be dead!

FISHERMAN: What?

SECOND DEMON: I am a demon!

FISHERMAN: One of the good ones?

SECOND DEMON: No!

FISHERMAN: But, demon, you're free, thanks to me. Are you gonna reward me?

SECOND DEMON: No! For two hundred years, I said to myself, whoever frees me from this bottle, I will shower them with treasure. But two hundred years passed, then hundreds more, but no-one set me free. So I raged and snorted and said to myself, if anyone ever opens this bottle … I will grant them a wish.

FISHERMAN: A wish?

SECOND DEMON: Yes. Which way do you wish to *die?*

KING SHAHRAYAR *enjoys seeing the* FISHERMAN *tormented.*

FISHERMAN: Shame on you. I did you a good turn. Why repay me with an evil one?

SECOND DEMON: Would you like scorpions to sting you?

FISHERMAN: Please, demon. You should reward me.

SECOND DEMON: Lions to maul you?

FISHERMAN: Don't deprive my children of me.

SECOND DEMON: Vultures to peck you to pieces?

FISHERMAN: If you destroy me, God will destroy you.

SECOND DEMON: Chose your death!

The FISHERMAN *thinks.*

FISHERMAN: Demon. That bottle, I reckon you weren't really in there. It's not big enough. Not even for just your feet.

SECOND DEMON: I was in that bottle for thousands of years!

FISHERMAN: No you weren't.

SECOND DEMON: Yes I was!

FISHERMAN: Impossible. How would your body fit?

SECOND DEMON: Don't you believe me?

FISHERMAN: No.

SECOND DEMON: Oh yeah? I'll show you, buster!

The DEMON *turns back into a column of smoke and re-enters the bottle.*

[*From inside the jar*] So! Do you believe me now?

The FISHERMAN *clamps the stopper on the bottle.*

FISHERMAN: Gotcha!

SECOND DEMON: Poo! You diddled me!

FISHERMAN: Yep. And now, back you go, into the ocean.

SECOND DEMON: Don't! Please!

FISHERMAN: You were gonna kill me!

SECOND DEMON: No. I was just joking. Honest.

FISHERMAN: Have a nice flight.

SECOND DEMON: Fisherman! Listen! If you destroy me, God will destroy you. He will!

The FISHERMAN *thinks.*

FISHERMAN: Demon. Our situation reminds me of the story of King Yunan and Professor Duban. You see, King Yunan …

The FISHERMAN *invites* KING SHAHRAYAR *to become* KING YUNAN.

KING SHAHRAYAR: King?

It is appropriate that only he play the role of a king, so he accepts.

Yes. Why not? I can play a king. King who?

FISHERMAN: Yunan. He reigned over the most beautiful city in all of Persia. He had wealth, wives, and a wonderful palace. Other kings envied him, until … he got a bad rash all over his body.

The SMUGGLES *stick red spots all over* KING YUNAN's *body.*

An icky, ugly, terrible rash that none of his doctors could fix. He lost his appetite, was always rude and cruel and itchy, until one day, a wise man called Professor Duban paid him a visit.

A SMUGGLE *becomes* PROFESSOR DUBAN.

PROFESSOR DUBAN: Your Majesty. Your condition is shocking. But I read Greek, Persian, Turkish, Arabic and Hebrew. I've studied science, philosophy and history. I know poetry and the healing lore of plants. I'm full of remedies, and can cure you without any potion or ointment.

KING YUNAN: You can?

PROFESSOR DUBAN: Yes.

KING YUNAN: If you can cure me, I will shower you in treasure and make you my lifelong friend.

PROFESSOR DUBAN: Splendid. Now, take this bat into the playground and play cricket. Hit the ball and run about until you laugh and sweat. If you do this, I promise, it will cure your affliction.

KING YUNAN: But who will I play cricket with?

PROFESSOR DUBAN: The peasants.

KING YUNAN: Peasants! But I'm a king! Peasants carry germs!

PROFESSOR DUBAN: With respect, My Lord, it is *you* who is contagious. Let the game begin!

The SMUGGLES, SHAHRAZAD *and* DINARZAD *become dispirited* PEASANTS *playing catch.*

PEASANTS: Catch catch
　Practice for a match
　That we can't play
　Till we get a bat …

　　KING YUNAN approaches and holds up his bat. The PEASANTS
　　are fearful at first. A PEASANT *throws the ball to him and* KING
　　YUNAN *hits it. They play.*

Catch catch
Ready for a match
That we can play
Now we have a bat …

　　The PEASANTS *play cricket and run around* KING YUNAN, *pulling off his spots.*

Look look
At the cruel king
His blotches are gone
No spots on his skin.

　　KING YUNAN *falls down sweaty and exhausted and happy. The*
　　PEASANTS *exit.*

PROFESSOR DUBAN: Your Majesty. Your skin is clean. Your complexion
　is clear.

　　KING YUNAN *stands and inspects his skin. He embraces*
　　PROFESSOR DUBAN.

KING YUNAN: Professor! You did it! Without any potion or ointment.
　Adviser! Where's my adviser?

　　A SMUGGLE *becomes* ADVISER TO KING YUNAN.

ADVISER TO KING YUNA: Yes, Your Majesty?
KING YUNAN: Bring clever Professor Duban a sparkling robe of honour.
　Send jewels to his wife and toys to his kids, and fulfil all his wishes.
　And bring a feast. I'm famished. Professor!
PROFESSOR DUBAN: Yes, Your Majesty?
KING YUNAN: Sweet, wise, wonderful Professor! You're a genius. Be
　my constant companion, my lifelong friend, and teach me everything
　you know. Bring on the Bollinger!

PROFESSOR DUBAN: Oh, champagne!

The ADVISER TO KING YUNAN *is seething with jealousy.*

ADVISER TO KING YUNAN: Your Majesty. All that sweating with the peasants has made you messy. Allow me to wash you. I wouldn't want you to get sick again.

KING YUNAN: Yes. Professor? I pong. Excuse me.

The ADVISER TO KING YUNAN *takes* KING YUNAN *aside and washes him.*

Look! No more disease or sores …

ADVISER TO KING YUNAN: Your Majesty.

KING YUNAN: … or scars or warts or carbuncles.

ADVISER TO KING YUNAN: The professor is your enemy.

KING YUNAN: What?

ADVISER TO KING YUNAN: The man you pamper is a spy.

KING YUNAN: Preposterous! His good deed proves that he's the most faithful, the most deserving, the dearest of all the people I know.

ADVISER TO KING YUNAN: But think, My King. He fixed you up by putting something in your hand. He could kill you just as easily, couldn't he?

KING YUNAN: You're jealous.

ADVISER TO KING YUNAN: Suspicious. He hasn't harmed me. But think of all the ways he might harm you.

KING YUNAN: Yes … If this professor has the power to cure me … he must have the power to kill me too. You're right. He's here to plot my destruction. What should I do?

ADVISER TO KING YUNAN: Kill him before he has a chance to kill you.

KING YUNAN: Yes. This instant. Professor!

PROFESSOR DUBAN: Yes, O happy King?

KING YUNAN: Prepare for your death.

PROFESSOR DUBAN: Excuse me? I did you a good turn. Why repay me with an evil one?

ADVISER TO KING YUNAN: Because you're a spy!

KING YUNAN: Here to steal from me and plot my death. So I must kill you before you kill me.

PROFESSOR DUBAN: Your Majesty. You are under the spell of the wrong story.

KING YUNAN: Executioner!

A SMUGGLE *becomes the* SECOND EXECUTIONER.

PROFESSOR DUBAN: Spare me, and God will spare you. Destroy me and God will destroy you.

KING YUNAN: Proceed!

The SECOND EXECUTIONER *raises his axe.*

PROFESSOR DUBAN: Wait. Kill me, if you must. But first, let me donate my scientific books to a great library. I have a particular book called *The Secret of Secrets.*

KING YUNAN: *The Secret of Secrets*?

PROFESSOR DUBAN: Yes.

KING YUNAN: Intriguing!

PROFESSOR DUBAN: I'd like to give it to you, Your Majesty, for safekeeping …

KING YUNAN: Very well. Yes. Where is it?

The SECOND EXECUTIONER *lowers his axe.* PROFESSOR DUBAN *pulls a book out of his pocket and gives it to* KING YUNAN.

PROFESSOR DUBAN: Here it is. When my head is cut off, open the book. Inside you will find the secret of secrets. But spare me and God will spare you. Destroy me and God will destroy you.

KING YUNAN: But I must know the secret of secrets. Proceed!

The SECOND EXECUTIONER *raises the axe.*

PROFESSOR DUBAN: You are warned.

KING YUNAN: Off with his head!

The SECOND EXECUTIONER *chops off* PROFESSOR DUBAN*'s head. It becomes* QUEEN SAHAR*'s head and floats into the air.* KING SHAHRAYAR *is shocked. He only barely manages to finish his portrayal of* KING YUNAN. *Her song and his dialogue overlap.*

QUEEN SAHAR: [*singing*] How long will you hurt
    Those who mean no harm …?

KING YUNAN: Now … yes … the secret of secrets. What is it?

KING YUNAN *tries to open the book. He licks his fingers, and with difficulty, opens some of the stuck pages.*

QUEEN SAHAR: [*singing*] You play with people's lives
    Like it is all a game …

KING YUNAN: The secret. Where is the …?

> KING YUNAN *keeps licking his fingers to open the book. He heaves and sways.*

The pages, they're blank … but … fingers taste … icky … feel icky …

QUEEN SAHAR: [*singing*] You are now
>> Left poisoned
>> Like our future.

KING YUNAN: Feeeel … arghhh.

> KING YUNAN *and* QUEEN SAHAR's *head succumb to death. The* SMUGGLES *revert to the characters in 'The Tale of the Fisherman and the Demon'.*

FISHERMAN: So, demon!

> KING SHAHRAYAR *returns to his own character, a little shaken.*

Consider this story. I was kind to you, but you wanted to kill me. So back you go, into the ocean.

SECOND DEMON: But, fisherman! If you destroy me, God will destroy you. He will! You said so, in your story. Let me out? Please?

FISHERMAN: No. You'll murder me.

SECOND DEMON: No. I'll make you rich. Very extremely rich. If you set me free.

FISHERMAN: You're just playing silly buggers.

SECOND DEMON: I'm not. I'm a demon of my word. This time, I will reward you. I promise.

> *The* FISHERMAN *thinks, then removes the stopper.*

> *The bottle shakes. The* FISHERMAN *drops it and leaps back as a column of smoke rises from the bottle. The smoke becomes the* SECOND DEMON, *played by a* SMUGGLE. *The* SECOND DEMON *kicks the bottle into the sea.*

Rejoice and be glad! For soon, you will be rich! Fisherman! Cast your net!

FISHERMAN: What? Again?

SECOND DEMON: Yes.

FISHERMAN: It's no use. The sea, it's too polluted.

SECOND DEMON: It's under a spell. Trust me. I know what I'm doing.

FISHERMAN: I hope so.

The FISHERMAN *casts his net.*

> [*Singing*] I cast my net
> Into the sea
> For a fourth time
> What will I find?

The FISHERMAN *hauls in his net.* COLOURED FISH *(a white fish, a red fish, a blue fish and a yellow fish) leap out and swim around him.*

Pretty fish! Do they taste good?

SECOND DEMON: No. They taste like people.

FISHERMAN: Why?

SECOND DEMON: Because they are people.

> *The* COLOURED FISH *sing.*

FISH: [*singing*] In a busy city
> We lived in peace
> Muslim, Hindu, Christian, Jew
> Until our streets
> Were turned into a sea
> Until our people
> Were turned into fish.

FISHERMAN: What horrible creature would cast such a spell?

SECOND DEMON: Me. When I rebelled against King Solomon the Prophet. This sea was a beautiful city, full of gardens, markets and fields. Until I got mad one day and changed it.

> *The* COLOURED FISH *sing.*

FISH: [*singing*] Turn that sea
> Back into streets
> Turn us fish
> Back into people
> We will crown
> The soul who saves us
> Muslim, Hindu, Christian, Jew.

FISHERMAN: Demon. Since I freed you *twice*, will you now free them?

SECOND DEMON: Yes.

> *The* SECOND DEMON *utters an incantation.*

If these fish are real fish
Let them stay fish
But if these fish are under my spell
Let them change back into people
By the will of the Creator of Everything.

> *The four* COLOURED FISH *turn into people and rejoice.*

SHAHRAZAD: And so, thanks to the kindness the fisherman showed the demon, the people crowned him king of their beautiful city …

KING SHAHRAYAR: A fisherman, a *king*?

> KING SHAHRAYAR *stoops in a mock bow.* SHAHRAZAD *takes the crown from his head, and crowns the* FISHERMAN.

SHAHRAZAD: … and he became one of the richest men of his time.

> KING SHAHRAYAR *is surprised. The* FISHERMAN, *who is a starving* SMUGGLE, *gravitates to the throne. He sits, eats, gathers food for later, tries on the king's sunglasses, et cetera.*

KING SHAHRAYAR: What a strange and amazing story.

SHAHRAZAD: Yes. But it's not as strange or amazing as the story of Ali Baba and the forty bandits.

KING SHAHRAYAR: Ali Baba and the forty bandits?

> *A rooster crows. Dawn breaks. The city outside bustles into action: traffic rumbles, vendors spruik, radios blare, children play.*

> *The* SMUGGLE *playing the* FISHERMAN *forgets to disappear into a crack in the wall. He remains on the throne, helping himself to the king's food.*

[*Aside*] By God, if I hurt her, I won't know the story of Ali Baba and the forty bandits. What will I do?

> *The* EXECUTIONER *enters with his axe. The* ADVISER *enters with a burial shroud.* SHAHRAZAD *and* DINARZAD *wait.*

Transition into …

The third daytime interlude:

KING SHAHRAYAR *ponders the stories he has heard, and looks at the* FISHERMAN *sitting on his throne, eating his food and drinking his wine. The sight of a lowly person on his throne shocks him. His first impulse is to command him to get off, but he hesitates. When the* FISHERMAN *notices the* KING, *he cowers, hands the* KING *his crown, and exits.* KING SHAHRAYAR *uncertainly puts the crown back on his head and unsteadily sits on his throne.*

Transition into ...

The next night.

KING SHAHRAYAR: Shahrazad. You may live another night.

> *The* ADVISER *and* EXECUTIONER *exit.*

But in the morning ...

SHAHRAZAD: Will you put me to death?

KING SHAHRAYAR: God Almighty willing. That is my vow, yes.

DINARZAD: Sister. If you're not too sleepy ...

KING SHAHRAYAR: ... tell us the tale about Ali Baba and the forty bandits?

SHAHRAZAD: With pleasure, O happy King... *Listen!*

> *At this word, the* SMUGGLES *come out of the cracks in the walls to play 'The Tale of Ali Baba and the Forty Bandits'.*

Once there was a woodchopper called Ali Baba. Every day Ali Baba chopped wood deep in the forest, and carried it back to sell in the city. He was very poor, but his brother, Qasim, was rich, greedy and selfish. Now, one day, Ali Baba borrowed a measuring pot from Qasim. When Ali Baba returned it, Qasim hit the roof. Because, stuck to the bottom of the pot, was a solid gold coin.

> *Two* SMUGGLES *become* ALI BABA *and* QASIM.

QASIM: Ali Baba! You sneaky little runt. Pretending to be flat broke. O me, O my, spare a little bread, brother? But what's this?

ALI BABA: Qasim!

QASIM: Cut the crap. This gold coin was stuck to that pot you borrowed.

ALI BABA: Was it?

QASIM: Which means, you must have *more* gold coins. More than you can count. More than me!

ALI BABA: I've had a bit of luck. Be happy for me.

QASIM: No. Show me. Or I'll tell the cops you're a robber. To throw you in the clink. Let me in! [*Yelling*] Ali Baba won't let his brother in! What's he hiding?

> ALI BABA *drags* QASIM *inside.*

ALI BABA: Be quiet.

QASIM: Show me, show me, show me!

> ALI BABA *pulls a bundle of gold coins out of his pocket.*

Where did you get this?

> ALI BABA *covers the money before* QASIM *can grab any.*

ALI BABA: Deep in the forest, there's a cave filled with stolen treasure.

QASIM: Treasure?

ALI BABA: I was chopping wood, when I heard horses. I hid up a tree, and saw forty men, with bulging saddlebags, ride up to this big rock. Their evil, ferocious captain, stood before the rock and said … 'Open sesame!'

KING SHAHRAYAR: Then what happened?

ALI BABA: The rock thundered and split open! The forty men marched in. When they came out and rode away, their saddlebags were empty.

KING SHAHRAYAR: They're bandits!

ALI BABA: They rob travellers!

QASIM: Bugger that. The rock opens if you say … 'Open sesame'?

ALI BABA: With the sound of thunder! Inside, there's stashed gold, the finest carpets, the lightest silk—

QASIM: And this is all you took?

ALI BABA: It's all I need. If I took more, the bandits would know it's missing, and track me down and kill me.

QASIM: Ha! Thanks, sucker!

KING SHAHRAYAR: Qasim! Be careful! Don't be too greedy!

> QASIM *hops onto a mule. He eventually gets the mule to co-operate, and heads off towards the cave.*

QASIM: Ali Baba is stupid! That's why he's so poor. Show you, buddy. Take as much as I want!

> QASIM *rides.*

Now where's that rock?

> QASIM *sees a rock, and stops the mule. He gets off and inspects the rock. He stands back.*

What was that word? Oh yes. Open sesame!

> *The rock splits apart with the sound of thunder.*

It worked!

QASIM *rushes inside the cave and is astonished. The* SMUGGLES *grab riches from King Shahrayar's chamber—silver, jewels, gold, carpets, silk—and swirl them around* QASIM.

Sweet loot! Dazzling stash! Centuries of stolen big bickies, all for me!

The rock slams shut with the sound of thunder. QASIM *doesn't notice. He feasts his eyes on the treasure.*

I'm rolling, stinking, filthy rich! But the bandits—better be quick. Grab what I can. Tomorrow I'll come back for more … and more … and more!

QASIM *fills his sack and drags it to the door. He realises he is shut in.*

Bottom. What was that word again? Open… lentil? No. That's not it … Open barley! Bugger. Open wheat? Open chickpea? Open pine nut?

A SMUGGLE *becomes the* BANDIT CAPTAIN.

BANDIT CAPTAIN: [*off*] Open sesame!

QASIM: Ah yes, that's it!

QASIM *freezes in fear. The rock splits apart with the sound of thunder to reveal the* BANDIT CAPTAIN.

BANDIT CAPTAIN: What are you doing in our secret cave?

QASIM: Fancy meeting you here. What's that?

Having distracted the BANDIT CAPTAIN, QASIM *makes a dash for freedom, but is blocked by the* 40 BANDITS.

BANDIT CAPTAIN: You sneaky trespassing thief! I'll chop you into four quarters and spread you around the cave. If any other fool discovers our den of treasure, the sight of your chopped-up body should scare them off!

The BANDIT CAPTAIN *draws his sword.*

QASIM: Help! Somebody …

The BANDIT CAPTAIN *chases, captures and quarters* QASIM. *He arranges his pieces on the ground and leaves.* KING SHAHRAYAR *is shocked by the killing. He sadly gathers the pieces of the body.*

KING SHAHRAYAR: Poor Qasim.

A SMUGGLE *becomes* ALI BABA. SHAHRAZAD *becomes* MAJANA. *They spread a shroud out on the ground.* KING SHAHRAYAR *places* QASIM's *pieces on the shroud. He and* ALI BABA *wrap them up, and hand them to* MAJANA.

ALI BABA: I went to the cave, and found the pieces of my brother. When it was dark, I placed him in my saddlebags, and snuck back home to do my duty and bury him.

MAJANA: Father. I'm worried. When the bandits discover that Qasim's body is missing, they'll want revenge.

ALI BABA: Yes, Majana, but we covered our tracks. They'll never find us.

MAJANA: We must still be careful. Come. Supper is ready.

MAJANA *leads* ALI BABA *and* KING SHAHRAYAR *to the throne area and serves them the King's own food as supper. The* BANDIT CAPTAIN *enters, leading a mule carrying forty oil jars. He wears a fake beard and is disguised as an oil merchant.*

BANDIT CAPTAIN: Good evening to all!

ALI BABA: Good evening!

BANDIT CAPTAIN: As you can see, I am a merchant. I've brought forty jars of oil from faraway, to sell at market in the morning. But, I've arrived too late to find lodgings.

ALI BABA: I am Ali Baba. You're welcome to spend the night here with us.

BANDIT CAPTAIN: Ali Baba. You're too kind. But my mule. Do you have room for him, too?

ALI BABA: Yes, my courtyard is big enough, and I have plenty of hay.

BANDIT CAPTAIN: You're very gracious.

KING SHAHRAYAR: Come in. You're just in time for supper.

BANDIT CAPTAIN: I'll just tie my mule up.

MAJANA: Let me help you.

BANDIT CAPTAIN: No! He gets stroppy around strangers. I must do it alone. I will be in directly. Go back to your supper. Go on.

ALI BABA, MAJANA, *and* KING SHAHRAYAR *go to the throne area. The* BANDIT CAPTAIN *leads his mule to the courtyard.*

ALI BABA: Majana. If you're not too sleepy, would you surprise our guest and dance for him?

MAJANA: Yes, father, with pleasure. I'll just change into my costume.

The BANDIT CAPTAIN *talks to the oil jars.* MAJANA *overhears this.*

BANDIT CAPTAIN: Comrades!

The lids on the oil jars lift: each jar contains a BANDIT.

40 BANDITS: Captain! Is it time to hideously mince and stab and poison those who know our secret?

BANDIT CAPTAIN: Not yet.

40 BANDITS: But they have discovered our den of treasure!

BANDIT CAPTAIN: And will not escape our vengeance. When everyone is asleep, I will give a signal. Then, jump out of the oil jars and hideously liquidate the lot of them.

40 BANDITS: Cut! Chop! Mangle! Kill! Hooray!

BANDIT CAPTAIN: Now shut up.

The 40 BANDITS *go back inside the jars and the lids shut.* MAJANA *hides.*

MAJANA: Liquidate? I must do something. Quickly. Before he gives the signal to kill us.

The BANDIT CAPTAIN *joins* ALI BABA *and* KING SHAHRAYAR.

ALI BABA: Friend! Join us for supper!

BANDIT CAPTAIN: It's late. We should sleep.

KING SHAHRAYAR: Later, later. Eat.

ALI BABA: These figs are delicious.

BANDIT CAPTAIN: Oh-oh, just one then.

ALI BABA and KING SHAHRAYAR *share the food.* MAJANA *comes out of hiding and goes to the jars. She disguises her voice.*

MAJANA: Comrades!

The lids on the oil jars lift: each jar contains a BANDIT.

40 BANDITS: Captain!

MAJANA uses the flame from her lamp to set the oil jars alight. The 40 BANDITS *cook.* MAJANA *exits.*

BANDIT CAPTAIN: I'm keeping you up.

KING SHAHRAYAR: More wine?

BANDIT CAPTAIN: I'm too pooped.

ALI BABA: And, gentlemen, you know what? I'm lucky. My family is tucked in, well fed. It is all the fortune I need.

BANDIT CAPTAIN: Good. Great. Time to turn in.

MAJANA *enters dancing.*

MAJANA: Guests! Loved ones!

BANDIT CAPTAIN: What is this?

MAJANA: Midnight revelry to honour our guest!

BANDIT CAPTAIN: But I must sleep.

ALI BABA: You must see Majana dance.

BANDIT CAPTAIN: It's late.

ALI BABA: She is amazing.

BANDIT CAPTAIN: No. Go to bed. Everybody, go to bed!

ALI BABA: Dance, my daughter! Please, captivate our guest.

MAJANA *dances for the* BANDIT CAPTAIN. *He soon overcomes his reluctance and is captivated by her. During her dance, she deftly steals his dagger and keeps him in tow.*

BANDIT CAPTAIN: Yes … lovely … very nice …

At the climax of the dance, MAJANA *stabs the* BANDIT CAPTAIN.

[*Dying*] For God's sake … go to bed.

He dies.

ALI BABA: Majana!

KING SHAHRAYAR: What have you done?

MAJANA: Saved us from the vengeful bandit captain.

MAJANA *takes off the* BANDIT CAPTAIN'*s false beard and holds it up.*

He was here to murder us.

ALI BABA: Just as you thought. But the other bandits. Quick, we must wake the family and run, before they—

MAJANA: Father. They are dead, too. Burnt inside the oil jars they were hiding in. They would have slaughtered us all. But now, we are safe.

ALI BABA *kisses* MAJANA *between the eyes.*

ALI BABA: Majana. Daughter of fortune! Light of my eyes! Glory to God who protects and gives abundance to the humble.

MAJANA: Father. Now only *we* know the secret of the cave. What shall we do?

ALI BABA: Let's bring the hidden treasure into the market, and use it to be kind to the poor, and hospitable to strangers.

KING SHAHRAYAR: What a blessing that would be for our city!

SHAHRAZAD *resumes her own character.*

SHAHRAZAD: And so, Ali Baba went to the cave and said …

ALI BABA: Open sesame!

SHAHRAZAD: He gave the treasure to anyone in need …

KING SHAHRAYAR *distributes some of his food and treasure to the* SMUGGLES *who then disappear into the cracks in the wall. All except for the* SMUGGLE *playing the* BANDIT CAPTAIN, *who remains lying on the ground.*

… and lived the rest of his life in happiness and peace.

KING SHAHRAYAR: What an amazing story.

SHAHRAZAD: Yes. But it's nothing compared to the story of the calligrapher and the demon.

KING SHAHRAYAR: Oh, please, Shahrazad …

He invites her to sit on a cushion at the foot of his throne. She does.

… what's the story of the calligrapher and the demon?

A rooster crows. Dawn breaks. The city outside bustles into action: traffic rumbles, vendors spruik, radios blare, children play.

[*Aside*] By God, if anything happens to sweet Shahrazad, I won't know the story of the calligrapher and the demon. What will I do?

SHAHRAZAD *falls asleep.*

The EXECUTIONER *enters with his axe. The* ADVISER *enters with a burial shroud.*

Transition into …

The fourth daytime interlude:

KING SHAHRAYAR *ponders the story and examines the* SMUGGLE *lying on the ground. The* SMUGGLE *is weak and exhausted.* KING SHAHRAYAR *helps the* SMUGGLE *to sit up and drink some water. The* SMUGGLE *revives and greedily drinks his fill.* KING SHAHRAYAR *uses his gown to wipe the* SMUGGLE'S *brow. The* SMUGGLE *turns his face to thank his helper, but realises he is staring into the face of the dreaded* KING SHAHRAYAR. *He scrambles and runs for his life back through a crack in the wall.* KING SHAHRAYAR *is alarmed at the terror he strikes into people's hearts.*

The EXECUTIONER *hoods his axe. The* ADVISER *smiles and folds up the burial shroud. They exit.*

Transition into ...

The next night.

KING SHAHRAYAR: Sweet Shahrazad. If you're not too sleepy, tell us one of your lovely tales to while away the night. The one about the calligrapher and the demon.

SHAHRAZAD: Yes, O happy King.

The SMUGGLES *confidently run out of cracks in the wall.*

SMUGGLES: *Listen!*

SMUGGLE ONE: The gracious King of Baghdad ...

KING SHAHRAYAR *steps into the story.*

... had two wise and gifted children.

SMUGGLE TWO: His son was a master calligrapher.

KING SHAHRAYAR *invites* DINARZAD *into the story.*

He wrote words with such beauty that anyone who read his writing lifted their hearts in praise.

SMUGGLE THREE: His daughter was an enchantress beyond measure.

KING SHAHRAYAR *invites* SHAHRAZAD *into the story.*

She spoke words with such wisdom that anyone who heard her opened their hearts with joy.

SMUGGLE ONE: One day, the son left to visit the King of India.

KING SHAHRAYAR *takes a ring off his finger and gives it to the* CALLIGRAPHER.

KING SHAHRAYAR: Here is a precious gift for the king. Thank him for his hospitality, and travel lightly in his land.

KING SHAHRAYAR *kisses the* CALLIGRAPHER.

KING OF BAGHDAD'S DAUGHTER: Farewell, beloved brother.

The KING OF BAGHDAD'S DAUGHTER *kisses the* CALLIGRAPHER.

CALLIGRAPHER: Farewell.

The CALLIGRAPHER *mounts his horse.*

KING OF BAGHDAD: Return to us safely.

CALLIGRAPHER: I will.

> *The* CALLIGRAPHER *gallops away. As he travels, the* SMUGGLES, *the* KING, *and* SHAHRAZAD *grab items from the king's chamber and carry them across the stage, to represent passing scenery and landmarks. When the Taj Mahal appears, the* CALLIGRAPHER *can't resist. He stops to take his picture in front of it. He mounts his horse and rides on, past more scenery and landmarks, then stops for a drink.*

> *Two* SMUGGLES *become* HIGHWAY ROBBERS *hiding behind a tree. They ambush him, and beat him. They steal his ring, get on his horse, and gallop away. A* SMUGGLE *becomes a* TAILOR *and helps the* CALLIGRAPHER *who is dazed and hurt.*

TAILOR: Foreign riffraff!

CALLIGRAPHER: What?

TAILOR: Highway robbers, the lot of them! Look at you. You're black and blue.

CALLIGRAPHER: Am I?

TAILOR: Here. Let me help. You local?

CALLIGRAPHER: My horse …

TAILOR: Bolted, probably. Locals have to stick together …

CALLIGRAPHER: The gift …

TAILOR: 'Cause riffraff breed like rabbits.

CALLIGRAPHER: I had a precious gift.

TAILOR: Gift? Are you a stranger?

CALLIGRAPHER: I'm a calligrapher from Baghdad …

TAILOR: Strangers are strange!

CALLIGRAPHER: … on my way to meet the King of India.

TAILOR: Strangers are dangerous!

CALLIGRAPHER: Where am I?

TAILOR: You're trespassing. Here uninvited. But not for long.

> *The* TAILOR *turns into a* THIRD DEMON.

CALLIGRAPHER: Oh no. Not *another* demon.

> *The* THIRD DEMON *grabs the* CALLIGRAPHER *and flies through the air.*

Where are you taking me?

The THIRD DEMON *dives back to earth and sets the* CALLIGRAPHER *down near the seaside.*

THIRD DEMON: Riffraff! Open your eyes!

CALLIGRAPHER: Oh. The sea! Are you going to drown me?

THIRD DEMON: No.

CALLIGRAPHER: Thank goodness.

THIRD DEMON: I'm going to turn you into a gorilla.

The THIRD DEMON *takes some sand, sprinkles it over the* CALLIGRAPHER, *and utters an incantation.*

If this man is local man
Let him stay a man
But if this man is from far away
Let him abandon his shape
And take on the form of a hairy ape.

The CALLIGRAPHER *becomes an* APE. *The* THIRD DEMON *flies away. The* APE *weeps. Other* SMUGGLES *become a* SEA CAPTAIN *and* MERCHANT *sailing on the bridge of a ship. The* APE *sees the ship, leaps around and runs back and forth to signal it.*

MERCHANT: Captain? What's that thing on shore, acting the ape? Is it a man?

SEA CAPTAIN: Ah! It's a strange manner of a man. Possibly a damsel.

MERCHANT: A damsel in distress?

SEA CAPTAIN: Ah! The high seas is full of highfalutin' things! I'm for picking the bugger up.

MERCHANT: But, captain, your ship's full of my costly cargo. What if you hit a reef and sink?

SEA CAPTAIN: Ah! Then it's Davey Jones' locker for the lot of us. Full steam ahead!

The SEA CAPTAIN *turns the ship and sails to shore.*

MERCHANT: No! Don't pick him up. I'll report you. Have you sacked!

They land, weigh anchor and disembark.

SEA CAPTAIN: Ah! Matey! Here we are. At your aid and rescue!

The APE *flings himself into the* SEA CAPTAIN*'s arms.*

MERCHANT: It's an ape.

SEA CAPTAIN: Ah! But quite a bright one to catch our eye like he did.

MERCHANT: My costly cargo, risked for a gorilla?

SEA CAPTAIN: Ah! God's creatures is all the same to me. Particularly one in distress. Welcome aboard, matey!

MERCHANT: No. I want him shot! Left to drown!

The APE *appeals to the* SEA CAPTAIN *for protection.*

SEA CAPTAIN: Ah! Sea captains never leave stranded souls stranded. All aboard!

MERCHANT: He stinks! He's bad luck! And anyway, he probably sunk his own boat to get your attention.

SEA CAPTAIN: Ah! Look, you pipsqueak. I run a hospitable ship. Turn *my* friend into *your* enemy, and you'll find yourself floating facedown in a barrel of pickled pork. Got it?

MERCHANT: Got it. Yes, captain. Welcome aboard … ape.

A MESSENGER *runs up to them.*

MESSENGER: Wait! All hands on deck must write a word for the king!

SEA CAPTAIN: Ah! Steady on, matey! Now which king would this be?

MESSENGER: The King of Baghdad. His beloved son is a master calligrapher. But he's travelling to India, and will be gone for years. So I must find a *new* Calligrapher to the King. Here is a scroll. Everyone must write a word. Who's first?

SEA CAPTAIN: Ah! Count me out. I'm illegitimate. Can't spell.

MERCHANT: Oh, I can. I practise my signature constantly. My style is expressive, but extremely neat, with the correct slant, and …

The APE *snatches the scroll and pen.*

Hey! He's gonna rip it. Chew it up! Give it here, you weaselly, wormy, stinky little …

The APE *unfurls the scroll and writes on it.*

SEA CAPTAIN: Ah! Shiver me timbers.

MESSENGER: Wow! Each letter is exquisite!

SEA CAPTAIN: What's he written?

MESSENGER: It's … *poetry.*

Transition into …

The KING OF BAGHDAD *and the* KING OF BAGHDAD'S DAUGHTER *talk to the* MESSENGER *who is showing them the writing on the scroll.*

KING OF BAGHDAD: Poetry?

KING OF BAGHDAD'S DAUGHTER: Father. This is amazing.

MESSENGER: Unbelievable, yes, but with my own eyes, I saw him write it.

KING OF BAGHDAD: Give this ape a sparkly sash of honour and bring him to the palace.

MESSENGER: Yes, Your Majesty.

KING OF BAGHDAD: If this ape's calligraphy is as good as my son's, who cares what shape he comes in?

The APE *enters. He bows before the* KING.

KING OF BAGHDAD'S DAUGHTER: Astonishing!

KING OF BAGHDAD: He has my son's manners at least!

KING OF BAGHDAD'S DAUGHTER: He has your son's eyes, too.

KING OF BAGHDAD: Mr Ape. I'm the King of Baghdad. Welcome to our city. You are here to write for me, I believe.

The APE *nods and brandishes a pen.*

Mr Ape. Please, write whatever is on your mind.

The APE *writes on the scroll. The* KING *reads, assembling the letters aloud into words.*

[*Reading*] 'Let the King of Baghdad know … that I am the King of Baghdad's… *son* …'

KING OF BAGHDAD'S DAUGHTER: Bewitched.

KING OF BAGHDAD: My son?

KING OF BAGHDAD'S DAUGHTER: I knew it.

KING OF BAGHDAD: Who did this?

KING OF BAGHDAD'S DAUGHTER: A demon, one of the wicked ones.

KING OF BAGHDAD: My dear daughter. You are an enchantress beyond measure. Surely, you have the power to change an animal into a man again.

KING OF BAGHDAD'S DAUGHTER: Yes, O happy King. I will give it my all.

The KING OF BAGHDAD'S DAUGHTER *draws a circle around the* KING *and the* APE.

You'll be safe inside the circle.

She summons all her courage.

Demon of hard and brutal hearts
I summon you here
To defy your black art.

Thunder and lightning. The earth trembles, and everything turns dark.

The FINAL DEMON *appears, a multi-headed monster played by three actors. It battles fiercely with the* KING OF BAGHDAD'S DAUGHTER. *The* APE *steps out of the circle to help, but is wounded and falls to the ground. The* KING OF BAGHDAD'S DAUGHTER *splits the* FINAL DEMON *into three pieces, but the pieces fight on separately. She is badly wounded, but defeats the pieces, one by one.*

The demon ... My Lord ... is defeated.

She staggers over to the KING *and says a spell over him.*

If the Almighty created this beast as a beast
Then let him stay a beast
But if this beast is under a treacherous spell
Let him change back into human being
By the will of the Creator of Everything.

The KING OF BAGHDAD'S DAUGHTER *dies and falls to the ground. Pause.* KING SHAHRAYAR *steps out of the story. He surveys the bodies that surround him, and faces the human cost of his actions.*

KING SHAHRAYAR: Shahrazad! Stand up.

SHAHRAZAD *stands before* KING SHAHRAYAR. *The* SMUGGLES *start to flee.*

Smuggles! Stop where you are.

They stop, terrified.

O, daughter of fortune, light of my eyes. The spell of the wrong story has been broken by you ... I beheaded my beloved queen. I locked the Smuggles in the dungeon, and vowed to kill every last one of them. That vow, I see, was the vow of a beast. I, King Shahrayar, break this bad vow. Smuggles, you are free. Strangers who seek help are welcome in this land. And sweet, wise, wonderful Shahrazad. You're a genius. Be my constant companion, my lifelong friend, and teach me everything you know. Bring on the Bollinger!

SMUGGLES: Yes! O happy King!

They celebrate and dance. QUEEN SAHAR'*s head enters, singing a celebration song.*

QUEEN SAHAR: [*singing*] We can trust the days
             Our hearts can be changed
             We can see the time
             When strangers become friends
             We are now
             Rejoicing
             At our future.

                    THE END